Chr

To a very dear
friend a

Merry Christmas
The Sikers

JOHN F. KENNEDY:

WORDS TO REMEMBER

John F. Kennedy:
Words to Remember

WITH A FOREWORD BY
ROBERT F. KENNEDY

Color Illustrations
by Frank V. Szasz

HALLMARK EDITIONS

Edited by Edward Lewis

and Richard Rhodes

The story of history is properly more than a succession of dates and events, of crisis and controversy. It is illuminated, at its best, by the acts and words of its participants.

I am pleased, therefore, that Hallmark is publishing this small volume. In these words of President Kennedy, we share once again the events—here and abroad—of his administration. Here are the tones of those struggles—for peace, for civil rights, for a better life for our people—whose echoes move us still, and shall always remain our concern.

Robert F. Kennedy

The stories of past courage can define that ingredient—they can teach, they can offer hope, they can provide inspiration. But they cannot supply courage itself. For this each man must look into his own soul.

In such a time as today the limits of human endeavor become more apparent than ever. We cannot depend solely on our material wealth, on our military might, on our intellectual skill or physical courage to see us safely through the seas that we must sail in the months and years to come. Along with all of these we need faith.

The guiding principle and prayer of this Nation has been, is now, and shall ever be "In God We Trust."

This nation—not Russia—is still the land of the free. And that, in the last analysis, is going to make the difference.

Peace does not rest in charters and covenants alone. It lies in the hearts and minds of all people. And in this world no act, no pact, no treaty, no organization can hope to preserve it without the support and the wholehearted commitment of all people.

In whatever arena of life one may meet the challenge of courage, whatever may be the sacrifices he faces if he follows his conscience — the loss of his friends, his fortune, his contentment, even the esteem of his fellow men — each man must decide for himself the course he will follow.

The meaning of courage, like political motivations, is frequently misunderstood. Some enjoy the excitement of its battle, but fail to note the implications of its consequences. Some admire its virtues in other men and other times, but fail to comprehend its current potentialities.

Without belittling the courage with which men have died, we should not forget those acts of courage with which men have *lived.*

To be courageous requires no exceptional qualifications, no magic formula, no special combination of time, place and circumstance. It is an opportunity that sooner or later is presented to us all.

The courage of life is often a less dramatic spectacle than the courage of a final moment; but is no less a magnificent mixture of triumph and tragedy.

In every celebration of ending and beginning there is both the remembrance of tribulation and the anticipation of good. There is, too, the knowledge that suffering must make both a people and a man more certain of the right, while triumph brings with it the command to respect the right.

Some say that they are tiring of this task, or tired of world problems and their complexities, or tired of hearing those who receive our aid disagree with us. But are we tired of living in a free world?

In the days ahead, only the very courageous will be able to make the hard and unpopular decisions necessary for our survival in the struggle with a powerful enemy—an enemy with leaders who need give little thought to the popularity of their course, who need pay little tribute to the public opinion they themselves manipulate, and who may force, without fear of retaliation at the polls, their citizens to sacrifice present laughter for future glory.

We know now that freedom is more than the rejection of tyranny, that prosperity is more than an escape from want, that partnership is more than a sharing of power. These are all, above all,

8

great human adventures.... We are called to a great new mission. It is not a mission of arbitrary power.... The mission is to create a new social order, founded on liberty and justice, in which men are the masters of their fate, in which states are the servants of their citizens and in which all men and women can share a better life for themselves and their children.

However close we sometimes seem to that dark and final abyss, let no man of peace and freedom despair.

For of those to whom much is given, much is required. And when at some future date the high court of history sits in judgment on each of us, recording whether in our brief span of service we fulfilled our responsibilities to the state, our success or failure, in whatever office we hold, will be measured by the answers to four questions: First, were we truly men of courage...? Second, were we truly men of judgment...? Third, were we truly men of integrity...? Finally, were we truly men of dedication...?

If the self-discipline of the free cannot match the iron discipline of the mailed fist, in economic, political, scientific and all the other kinds of struggles as well as the military, then the peril to freedom will continue to rise.

Our programs must aim at expanding American productive capacity at a rate that shows the world the vigor and vitality of a free economy.

Any dangerous spot is tenable if men — brave men — will make it so.

Our foremost aim is the control of force, not the pursuit of force, in a world made safe for mankind. But whatever the future brings, I am sworn to uphold and defend the freedom of the American people, and I intend to do whatever must be done to fulfill that solemn obligation.

You can't have religious freedom without political freedom, and religious freedom has no significance unless it is accompanied by conviction.

Wherever we are, we must all, in our daily lives, live up to the age-old faith that freedom and peace walk together.

Just as the Family of Man is not limited to a single race or religion, neither can it be limited to a single city or country. The Family of Man is more than 3 billion strong. It lives in more than 100 nations.

Only the strength and progress and peaceful change that come from independent judgment and individual ideas can enable us to surpass that foreign ideology that fears free thought more than it fears hydrogen bombs.

While the Berlin wall is the most obvious and vivid demonstration of the failures of the Communist system, for all the world to see, we take no satisfaction in it, for it is an offense not only against history but an offense against humanity, separating families, dividing husbands and wives and brothers and sisters, and dividing a people who wish to be joined together.

A city does not become free merely by calling it a "free city." For a city or a people to be free requires that they be given the opportunity, without economic, political, or police pressure, to make their own choice and to live their own lives.

A man does what he must—in spite of personal consequences, in spite of obstacles and dangers and pressures—and that is the basis of all human morality.

When party and officeholder differ as to how the national interest is to be served, we must place first the responsibility we owe not to our party or even to our constituents but to our individual consciences.

We must present to the world a concept of freedom which has not been diluted by the evils of prejudice and discrimination. As Woodrow Wilson once said in an address on citizenship: "No amount of dwelling upon the idea of liberty and of justice will accomplish the object we have in view unless we ourselves illustrate the idea of justice and liberty."

Difficult days need not be dark. I think these are proud and memorable days in the cause of peace and freedom. . . . We have every reason to believe that our tide is running strong.

Together, let us build sturdy mansions of freedom, mansions that all the world can admire and copy, but that no tyrant can ever enter.

While maintaining our readiness for war, let us exhaust every avenue for peace. Let us always make clear our willingness to talk, if talk will help, and our readiness to fight, if fight we must.

Let us resolve to be the masters, not the victims, of our history, controlling our own destiny without giving way to blind suspicion and emotion.

The making of peace is the noblest work of God-fearing men.

It is the fate of this generation to live with a struggle we did not start, in a world we did not make. But the pressures of life are not always distributed by choice. And while no nation has ever faced such a challenge, no nation has ever been so ready to seize the burden and the glory of freedom.

This is a difficult fight. It is not easy. If it were easy, we would not be talking about it now. But all I am saying is that we are committing ourselves to the fight.

If we cannot end now our differences, at least we can help make the world safe for diversity. For in the final analysis our most basic common link is that we all inhabit this planet. We all breathe the same air. We all cherish our children's future. And we are all mortal.

When written in Chinese, the word "crisis" is

composed of two characters — one represents danger and one represents opportunity.

Let us not rest all our hopes on parchment and on paper. Let us strive to build peace, a desire for peace, a willingness to work for peace, in the hearts and minds of all of our people. I believe that we can. I believe the problems of human destiny are not beyond the reach of human beings.

The path we have chosen for the present is full of hazards, as all paths are, but it is the one most consistent with our character and courage as a nation and our commitments around the world. The cost of freedom is always high, but Americans have always paid it. And one path we shall never choose, and that is the path of surrender or submission.

America faces challenges greater than any which it has faced before. This is no time for complacency. This is no time to abandon the drive and the optimism and the imaginative creativity which have characterized this country since its birth. This is no time for timidity or doubt. This is a time for boldness and energy. This is a time for stouthearted men who can turn dreams into reality.

I believe in an America where the separation of church and state is absolute — where no Catholic prelate would tell the President how to act, and no Protestant minister would tell his parishioners for whom to vote — and where no man is denied public office merely because his religion differs from the President who might appoint him or the people who might elect him.

If we succeed in this country, if we make this a great country to live in, if we reflect our vitality and energy and strength around the world, then the cause of freedom is strengthened. But if we fail, all fail. If we stand still, freedom stands still.

It is only when the iron is hot that it can be molded. The iron of the new world being forged today is now ready to be molded. Our job is to shape it, so far as we can, into the world we want for ourselves and our children and for all men.

There was, in Korea, a young prisoner of war who was singled out of the line-up upon capture and asked his opinion of General Marshall. "General George C. Marshall," he replied, "is a great American soldier." Promptly a rifle butt knocked him to the ground. Then he was stood up again to face his captors — and again he was asked: "What do you think of General Marshall?" And again he gave the same steadfast reply — only this time there was no rifle butt, no punishment at all. They had tested his will, his courage to resist, his manhood — and now they knew where to classify him.

It is, I think, our intention to bear in mind the words of Lincoln during the darkest days of the Civil War. Many were fearful of the outcome and many were concerned about our survival, and when a delegation called on the President to express its fears, Lincoln told them of an experience of his youth. "One night in November," he said, "a shower of meteors fell from the clear night sky. A friend standing by was frightened. But I looked up and between the falling stars I saw the fixed stars beyond, shining serene in the firmament, and I said, 'Let us not mind the meteors, let us keep our eyes on the stars'." As we face a difficult and sometimes dangerous future, let us look beyond the falling meteors of the present and look to the steady stars that have guided this country through so many difficult times.

THE FIRST INAUGURAL ADDRESS

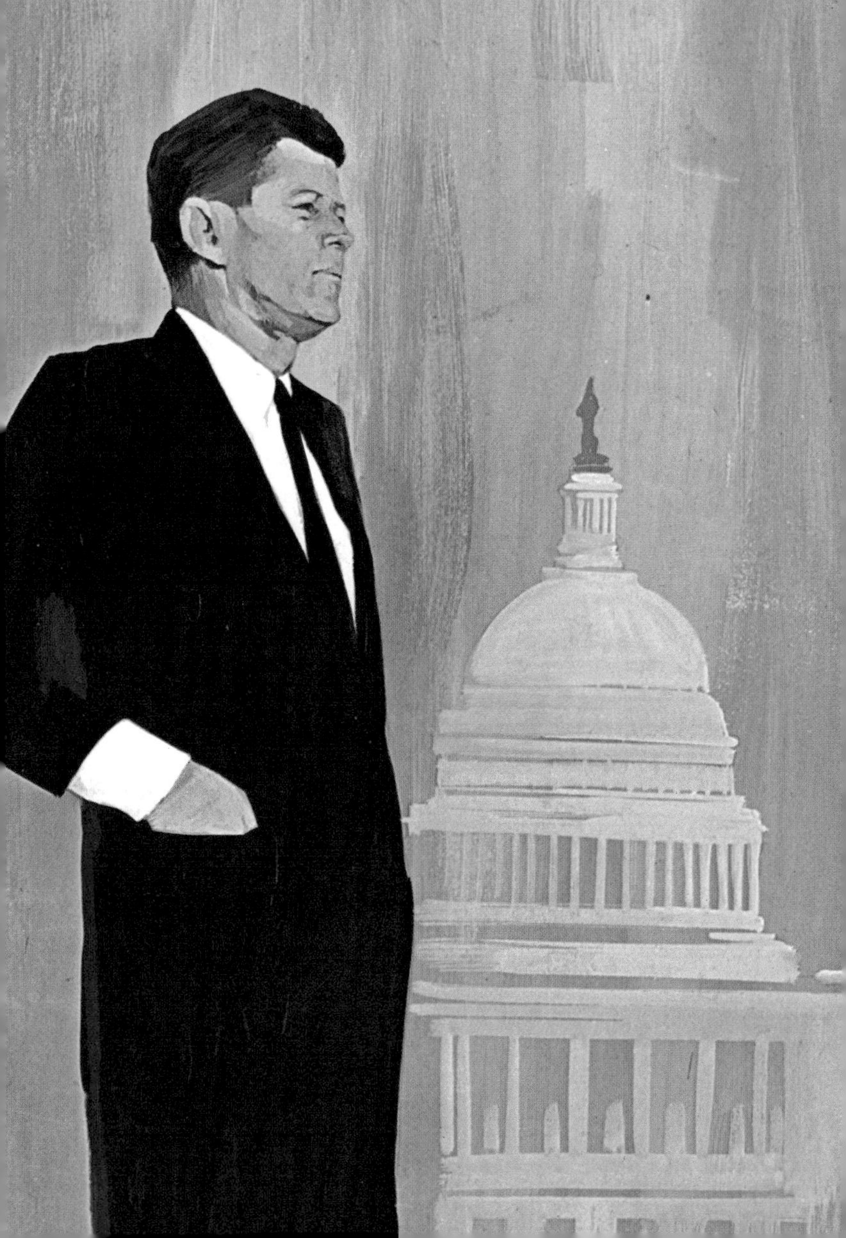

We observe today not a victory of party but a celebration of freedom — symbolizing an end as well as a beginning — signifying renewal as well as change. For I have sworn before you and Almighty God the same solemn oath our forebears prescribed nearly a century and three quarters ago.

The world is very different now. For man holds in his mortal hands the power to abolish all forms of human poverty and all forms of human life. And yet the same revolutionary beliefs for which our forebears fought are still at issue around the globe — the belief that the rights of man come not from the generosity of the state but from the hand of God.

We dare not forget today that we are the heirs of that first revolution. Let the word go forth from this time and place, to friend and foe alike, that the torch has been passed to a new generation of Americans — born in this century, tempered by war, disciplined by a hard and bitter peace, proud of our ancient heritage — and unwilling to witness or permit the slow undoing of those human rights to which this nation has always been committed, and to which we are committed today at home and around the world.

Let every nation know, whether it wishes us well or ill, that we shall pay any price, bear any burden, meet any hardship, support any friend, oppose any foe to assure the survival and the success of liberty.

This much we pledge — and more.

To those old allies whose cultural and spiritual origins we share, we pledge the loyalty of faithful friends. United, there is little we cannot do in a host of cooperative ventures. Divided, there is little we can do — for we dare not meet a powerful challenge at odds and split asunder.

To those new states whom we welcome to the ranks of the free, we pledge our word that one form of colonial control shall not have passed away merely to be replaced by a far more iron tyranny. We shall not always expect to find them supporting our view. But we shall always hope to find them strongly supporting their own freedom — and to remember that, in the past, those who foolishly sought power by riding the back of the tiger ended up inside.

To those peoples in the huts and villages of

half the globe struggling to break the bonds of mass misery, we pledge our best efforts to help them help themselves, for whatever period is required — not because the Communists may be doing it, not because we seek their votes, but because it is right. If a free society cannot help the many who are poor, it cannot save the few who are rich.

To our sister republics south of our border, we offer a special pledge — to convert our good words into good deeds — in a new alliance for progress — to assist free men and free governments in casting off the chains of poverty. But this peaceful revolution of hope cannot become the prey of hostile powers. Let all our neighbors know that we shall join with them to oppose aggression or subversion anywhere in the Americas. And let every other power know that this hemisphere intends to remain the master of its own house.

To that world assembly of sovereign states, the United Nations, our last, best hope in an age where the instruments of war have far outpaced the instruments of peace, we renew our pledge of support — to prevent it from becoming merely a forum for invective — to strengthen its shield of the new and the weak — and to enlarge the area in which its writ may run.

Finally, to those nations who would make themselves our adversary, we offer not a pledge but a request: that both sides begin anew the quest for peace, before the dark powers of destruction unleashed by science engulf all humanity in planned or accidental self-destruction.

We dare not tempt them with weakness. For only when our arms are sufficient beyond doubt can we be certain beyond doubt that they will never be employed.

But neither can two great and powerful groups of nations take comfort from our present course — both sides overburdened by the cost of modern weapons, both rightly alarmed by the steady spread of the deadly atom, yet both racing to alter that uncertain balance of terror that stays the hand of mankind's final war.

So let us begin anew — remembering on both sides that civility is not a sign of weakness, and sincerity is always subject to proof. Let us never negotiate out of fear. But let us never fear to negotiate.

Let both sides explore what problems unite us instead of belaboring those problems which divide us.

Let both sides, for the first time, formulate serious and precise proposals for the inspection and control of arms — and bring the absolute power to destroy other nations under the absolute control of all nations.

Let both sides seek to invoke the wonders of science instead of its terrors. Together let us explore the stars, conquer the deserts, eradicate disease, tap the ocean depths and encourage the arts and commerce.

Let both sides unite to heed in all corners of the earth the command of Isaiah — to "undo the heavy burdens...(and) let the oppressed go free."

And if a beachhead of cooperation may push back the jungle of suspicion, let both sides join in creating a new endeavor, not a new balance of power, but a new world of law, where the strong are just and the weak secure and the peace preserved.

All this will not be finished in the first one hundred days. Nor will it be finished in the first one thousand days, nor in the life of this Administration, nor even perhaps in our lifetime on this planet. But let us begin.

In your hands, my fellow citizens, more than mine, will rest the final success or failure of our course. Since this country was founded, each generation of Americans has been summoned to give testimony to its national loyalty. The graves of young Americans who answered the call to service surround the globe.

Now the trumpet summons us again — not as a call to bear arms, though arms we need — not as a call to battle, though embattled we are — but a call to bear the burden of a long twilight struggle, year in and year out, "rejoicing in hope, patient in tribulation" — a struggle against the common enemies of man: tyranny, poverty, disease and war itself.

Can we forge against these enemies a grand and global alliance, North and South, East and West, that can assure a more fruitful life for all mankind? Will you join in that historic effort?

In the long history of the world, only a few generations have been granted the role of defending freedom in its hour of maximum danger. I do not shrink from this responsibility — I welcome it. I do not believe that any of us would exchange places with any other people or any other generation. The energy, the faith, the devotion which we bring to this endeavor will light our country and all who serve it — and the glow from that fire can truly light the world.

And so, my fellow Americans: ask not what your country can do for you — ask what you can do for your country.

My fellow citizens of the world: ask not what America will do for you, but what together we can do for the freedom of man.

Finally, whether you are citizens of America or citizens of the world, ask of us here the same high standards of strength and sacrifice which we ask of you. With a good conscience our only sure reward, with history the final judge of our deeds, let us go forth to lead the land we love, asking His blessing and His help, but knowing that here on earth God's work must truly be our own.

Delivered January 20, 1961

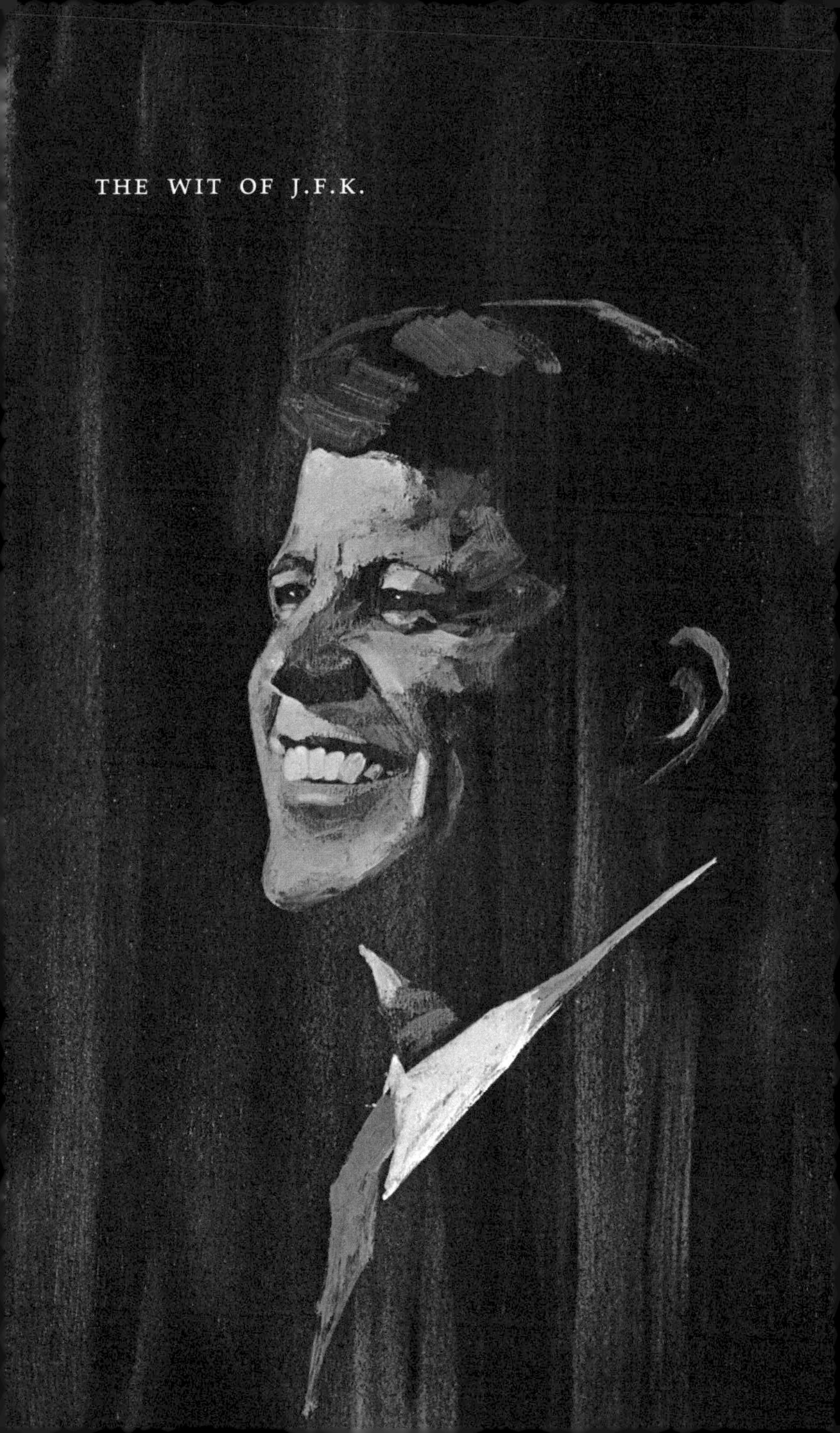
THE WIT OF J.F.K.

As Finley Peter Dunne's "Mr. Dooley" used to say, "Trust everyone, but cut the cards."

Americans want to be liked—and Senators are no exception.

I think it is appropriate that we begin the 1960 campaign right here in the State of California, and I think it is appropriate that we begin it on Labor Day weekend. The Republicans are all at the beach, but we are out here at this airport.

Mr. Nixon may be very experienced in kitchen debates. So are a great many other married men I know.

Question: "Senator, Governor Brown today issued a very optimistic statement. . . . Yet the field poll shows Nixon running ahead. . . . Which of these two experts do you believe?"
Answer: "I believe Governor Brown."

I hear that there are some Americans and some Democrats who say that they have now developed a wonderful arrangement in Washington. The Congress is Democratic and the President is Republican and nothing happens and isn't it wonderful.

I assume that your presence here indicates that you are all politicians. Artemus Ward from Massachusetts, my own state, 50 years ago said, "I am not a politician and my other habits are good, also."

There is a question of do I believe all Protestants are heretics. No, and I hope you don't believe all Catholics are.

President Truman told me the other night that his campaign train ran out of funds three times in 1948 and they had to come and get him.

A weekly newsmagazine with wide circulation featured a section entitled "Kennedy's Liberal Promises," and described me, and I quote, as the farthest-out liberal Democrat around, unquote. While I am not certain of the "beatnik" definition of "farthest-out," I am certain that this was not intended as a compliment.

Remark at a breakfast:
Looking at all you ladies and seeing what you have done with some of your distinguished officeholders, I recall an experience of the suffragettes who picketed the White House back during the First World War. The leader of the

suffragettes was arrested. As she was taken away in a truck, she turned to her girls and said, "Don't worry, girls. Pray to the Lord. *She* will protect you."

Our goal must be the fullest utilization of every drop and gallon of water in every river system in America, and it is a source of regret to me that the Potomac River, which flows by our Capital, is one of the most polluted rivers west of the Ganges. That is a long sentence, but you do get the idea.

The Vice President recently predicted that we would some day have a woman President. It might be discounted to a degree, because he was speaking at a women's college.

There is no city in the United States in which I get a warmer welcome and less votes than Columbus, Ohio.

On being President:
I have a nice home, the office is close by and the pay is good.

Mothers may still want their favorite sons to grow up to be President, but, according to a famous Gallup poll of some years ago, they do not want them to become politicians in the process.

Thomas Jefferson objected to George Washington because the Constitutional Convention had agreed to the founding of the Senate. He said, "Why is a Senate necessary?" And as you know, according to the story, Washington said, "Why do I pour my coffee in a cup? To cool it. So we need the Senate."

Those of you [students] who regard my profession of political life with some disdain should remember that it made it possible for me to move from being an obscure lieutenant in the United States Navy to Commander in Chief in 14 years, with very little technical competence.

More will be needed than good intentions, for we know where that paving leads.

We don't want to be like the leader in the French Revolution who said, "There go my people. I must find out where they are going so I can lead them."

The President bears the burden of the responsibility. The advisers may move on to new advice.

My experience in government...is that when things are noncontroversial, beautifully coordinated, and all the rest, it must be that not much is going on.

I share the feeling expressed by Prime Minister Melbourne, who, when irritated by the criticism of the then youthful historian T. B. Macaulay, remarked that he would like to be as sure of anything as Macaulay seemed to be of everything.

I want to express my great appreciation at the opportunity to be here with you, and to express my thanks to all of you for having attended this [Youth Fitness] Conference. I asked those members of the Cabinet who felt they were physically fit to come here today, and I am delighted that Mr. Udall and Mr. Robert Kennedy and Governor Ribicoff responded to the challenge.

Introducing astronaut Alan Shepard:
We have with us today the nation's number one television performer, who I think on last Friday morning secured the largest rating of any morning show in recent history.

A few years ago, at a diplomatic party in Moscow, Premier Khrushchev told the assembled guests about the Russian who suddenly began to run through the corridors of the Kremlin shouting: "Khrushchev is a fool. Khrushchev is a fool." He was sentenced, the Premier said, to 23 years in prison—"three for insulting the Party Secretary—and 20 for revealing a state secret."

They have offered to trade us an apple for an orchard. We don't do that in this country.

We cannot negotiate with those who say, "What's mine is mine and what's yours is negotiable."

I am the man who accompanied Jacqueline Kennedy to Paris, and I have enjoyed it.

I have been presented with this donkey by two young ladies down there for my daughter. My daughter has the greatest collection of donkeys. She doesn't even know what an elephant looks like. We are going to protect her from that knowledge.

Yesterday I was shown the Alamo and I was informed of all the brave deeds of all the Texans, of Bowie and Crockett and all the rest. So I said last night "Haven't you heard of Paul Revere?" They said, "Yes, he is the one who ran for help."

There is a story about a Texan who went to New York and told the New Yorker that he could jump off the Empire State Building and live. The Easterner said "Well, that would be an accident." He said "Suppose I did it twice?" The Easterner said "That would be an accident too." "Suppose I did it three times?" And the Easterner said, "That would be a habit."

At a dinner honoring all living Nobel Prize winners in the Western Hemisphere:
I want to tell you how welcome you are to the White House. I think this is the most extraordinary collection of talent, of human knowledge, that has ever been gathered together at the White House, with the possible exception of when Thomas Jefferson dined alone.

I actually came down here tonight to pay a debt of obligation to an old friend and faithful adviser. He and I came to the 80th Congress together, and have been associated for many years, and I regard him as one of my most valuable counselors in moments of great personal and public difficulty. In 1952, when I was thinking about running for the United States Senate, I went to the then Senator Smathers, and said, "George, what do you think?" He said, "Don't do it. Can't win. Bad year." In 1956 I was at the Democratic Convention, and I said—I didn't know whether I would run for Vice President or not, so I said, "George, what do you think?" "This is it. They need a young man. It's your chance." So I ran—and lost. And in 1960 I was wondering whether I ought to run in the West Virginia primary. "Don't do it. That state you can't possibly carry." And actually, the only time I really got nervous about the whole matter at Los Angeles, was just before the balloting, and George came up and he said, "I think it looks pretty good for you."

I spoke a year ago today, to take the Inaugural, and I would like to paraphrase a couple of statements I made that day by saying that we observe tonight not a celebration of freedom but a victory of Party, for we have sworn to pay off the same party debt our forebears ran up nearly a year and three months ago.

Our deficit will not be paid off in the next hundred days, nor will it be paid off in the first one thousand days, nor in the life of this Administration, nor, perhaps even in our lifetime on this planet, but let us begin—remembering that generosity is not a sign of weakness and that Ambassadors are always subject to Senate confirmation, for if the Democratic Party cannot be helped by the many who are poor, it cannot be saved by the few who are rich.

As General DeGaulle occasionally acknowledges America to be the daughter of Europe, so I am pleased to come to Yale, the daughter of Harvard. It might be said now that I have the best of both worlds, a Harvard education and a Yale degree.

I want to commend this idea of the $250 dinner. This is like that story of the award of prizes by the Moscow Cultural Center, the first prize being one week in Kiev and the second prize being two weeks. For $100 you get speeches; for $250 you don't get any speeches. You can't get bargains like that any more.

I used to wonder when I was a member of the House how President Truman got in so much trouble. Now I am beginning to get the idea. It is not difficult.

I got a letter, the nicest letter I have gotten, actually, since I have been in the White House, from an official of the Bethlehem Steel Company, saying, "You are even worse than Harry Truman."

34

We stand for freedom. That is our conviction for ourselves; that is our only commitment to others. No friend, no neutral and no adversary should think otherwise. We are not against any man — or any nation — or any system — except as it is hostile to freedom.

When I talked about the new frontier, I was not talking about the geography of this country.... I was talking about the spirit which has built our country, the kind of spirit which can build our country again.

The American, by nature, is optimistic. He is experimental, an inventor and a builder who builds best when called upon to build greatly.... This trait of the American character is our greatest single national asset.

For all America — its President and its people — the coming years will be a time of decision. We must decide whether we have reached our limit, or whether, in the words of Thomas Wolfe, "the true discovery of America is before us — the true fulfillment of our mighty and immortal land is yet to come."

Too often a project is undertaken in the excitement of a crisis and then it begins to lose its appeal as the problems drag on and the bills pile up. But we must have the steadfastness to see every enterprise through.

Our goal is not the victory of might, but the vindication of right; not peace at the expense of freedom, but both peace *and* freedom, here in this hemisphere, and around the world. God willing that goal will be achieved.

We can move forward with the confidence that is born of success and the skill that is born of experience. And as we move, let us take heart from the certainty that we are united not only by danger and necessity, but by hope and purpose as well.

It is our task in our time and in our generation to hand down undiminished to those who come after us, as was handed down to us by those who went before, the natural wealth and beauty which is ours.

There is no point in speaking out against the spread of Communism if we are unwilling to recognize which weapons are most needed in that struggle. There is no point in calling for vigorous action to protect our security if we are unwilling to pay the price.

We sometimes chafe at the burden of our obligations, the complexity of our decisions, the agony of our choices. But there is no comfort or security for us in evasion, no solution in abdication, no relief in irresponsibility.

I don't think there is any American who wants it said that in the days of his generation, when he bore responsibility as a citizen, the power shifted from the free world to that of the Communist. I don't want historians in 1970 to say that in the 1950's and 1960's the Communists made a decisive breakthrough.

Modern American capitalism, with its unique combination of public effort and private competitive enterprise, is dynamic, progressive, and still evolving. It may, from time to time, pause or show weakness. But it is still capable of greater heights than any Mr. Khrushchev has ever seen or imagined.

ON TECHNOLOGY AND THE ARTS

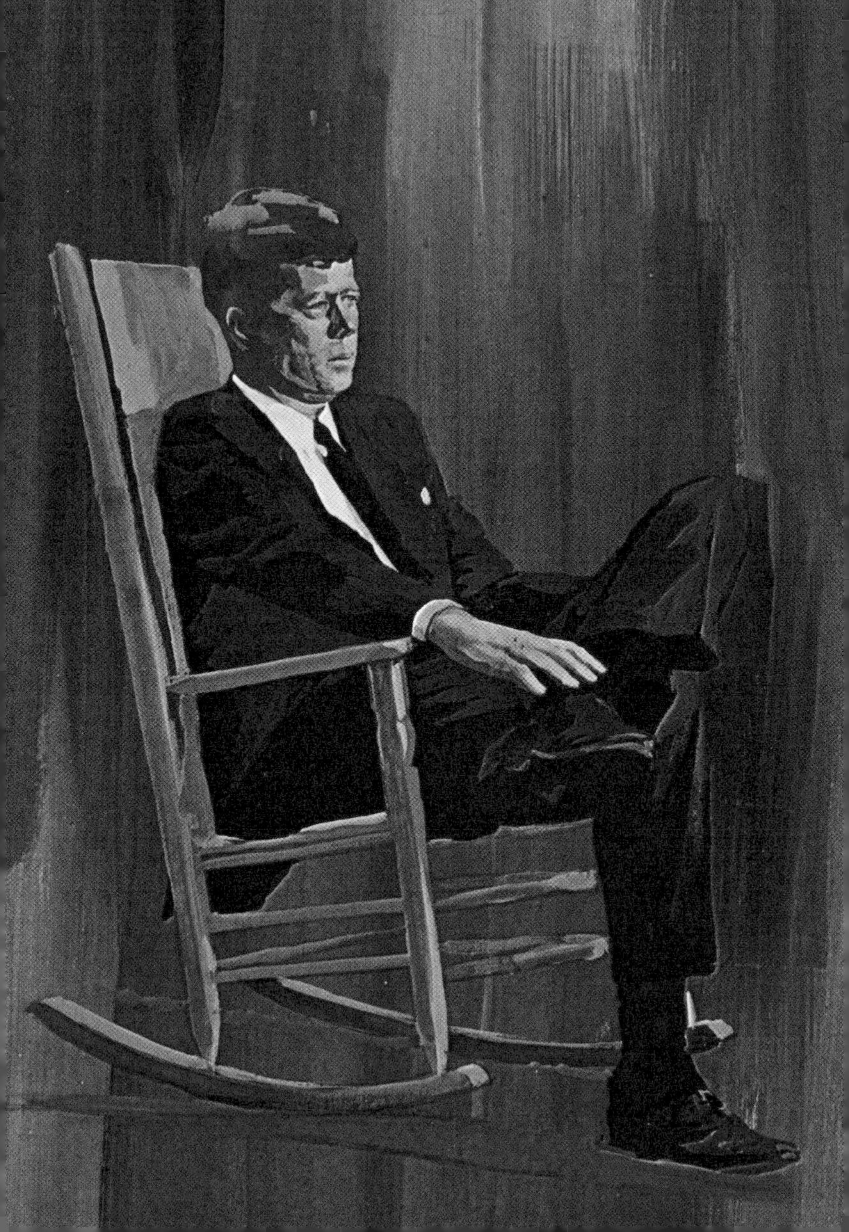

No man can fully grasp how far and how fast we have come, but condense, if you will, the fifty thousand years of man's recorded history in a time span of but a half century. Stated in these terms, we know very little about the first forty years, except that at the end of them advanced man had learned to use the skins of animals to cover himself.

Then about ten years ago, under this standard, man emerged from his caves to construct other kinds of shelter. Only five years ago man learned to write and use a cart with wheels. Christianity began less than two years ago. The printing press came this year, and then less than two months ago, during this whole fifty-year span of human history, the steam engine provided a new source of power. . . .

Last month electric lights and telephones and automobiles and airplanes became available. Only last week did we develop penicillin and television and nuclear power, and now if America's new spacecraft succeeds in reaching Venus, we will have literally reached the stars before midnight tonight.

This is a breathtaking pace, and such a pace cannot help but create new ills as it dispels old — new ignorance, new problems, new dangers. Surely the opening vistas of space promise high costs and hardships, as well as high reward.

The poet, the artist, the musician, continue the quiet work of centuries, building bridges of experience between peoples, reminding man of the universality of his feelings and desires and despairs, and reminding him that the forces that unite are deeper than those that divide.

The earth, the sea and the air are the concerns of every nation. And science, technology and education can be the ally of every nation.

We celebrate the past to awaken the future.

Our problems are man-made; therefore they can be solved by man.

Man can be as big as he wants. No problem of human destiny is beyond human beings. Man's reason and spirit have often solved the seemingly unsolvable, and we believe they can do it again.

Today we recognize increasingly the essentiality of artistic achievement. This is part, I think, of a nationwide movement toward excellence — a movement which had its start in the admiration of expertness and skill in our technical society, but which now demands quality in all realms of human achievement.

We know that science is indispensable — but we also know that science, if divorced from a knowledge of man and of man's ways, can stunt a civilization. And so the educated man reaches out for the experience which the arts alone provide. He wants to explore the side of life which expresses the emotions and embodies values and ideals of beauty.

Too often in the past, we have thought of the artist as an idler and dilettante and of the lover of arts as somehow sissy or effete. We have done both an injustice. The life of the artist is, in relation to his work, stern and lonely. He has labored hard, often amid deprivation, to perfect his skill. He has turned aside from quick success in order to strip his vision of everything secondary or cheapening. His working life is marked by intense application and intense discipline.

We must use time as a tool, not as a couch.

According to the ancient Chinese proverb, "A journey of a thousand miles must begin with a single step." My fellow Americans, let us take that first step. Let us, if we can, get back from the shadows of war and seek out the way of peace. And if that journey is one thousand miles, or even more, let history record that we, in this land, at this time, took the first step.

Our patience at the bargaining table is nearly inexhaustible, though our credulity is limited.

In short, we are neither "warmongers" nor "appeasers," neither "hard" nor "soft."

Let us debate colonialism in full, and apply the principle of free choice and the practice of free plebiscites in every corner of the globe.

The purpose of foreign policy is not to provide an outlet for our own sentiments of hope or indignation; it is to shape real events in a real world.

American agricultural abundance can be forged into both a significant instrument of foreign policy and a weapon against domestic hardship and hunger.

Unconditional war can no longer lead to unconditional victory.

Every nation has its own traditions, its own values, its own aspirations. Our assistance from time to time can help other nations preserve their independence and advance their growth, but we cannot remake them in our own image.

This is the side of the hill, not the top. The mere absence of war is not peace.

We shall need compromises in the days ahead, to be sure. But these will be, or should be, compromises of issues, not of principles.

Today no nation can build its destiny alone. The age of self-sufficient nationalism is over. The age of interdependence is here. The cause of Western European unity is based on logic and common sense. It is based on moral and political truth. It is based on sound military and economic principles, and it moves with the tide of history.

The hopes of all mankind rest upon us; not simply upon those of us in this chamber, but upon the peasant in Laos, the fisherman in Nigeria, the exile from Cuba, the spirit that moves every man and nation who shares our hopes for freedom and the future.

We seek to keep peace inside the non-Communist world, where many nations, all of them our friends, are divided over issues which weaken Western unity, which invite Communist intervention or which threaten to erupt into war.

The events and decisions of the next ten months may well decide the fate of man for the next 10,000 years. There will be no avoiding these events. There will be no appeal from these decisions.

If we were to treat foreign policy as merely a medium for delivering self-righteous sermons to supposedly inferior people, we would give up all thought of world influence or world leadership.

We meet here in an hour of grief and challenge. Dag Hammarskjold is dead. But the United Nations lives.

Compromise need not mean cowardice.

Today, this nation, conceived in revolution, nurtured in liberty, matured in independence, has no intention of abdicating its leadership in that worldwide movement for independence to any nation or society committed to systematic human suppression.

Any potential aggressor contemplating an attack on any part of the free world with any kind of weapons, conventional or nuclear, must know that our response will be suitable, selective, swift, and effective.

So I go to see Mr. Khrushchev in Vienna. I go as the leader of the greatest revolutionary country on earth. I know that there is in some areas of the world, and even in some parts of the United States, an image of us as a fixed society. That is not my view.

Where nature makes natural allies of us all, we can demonstrate that beneficial relations are possible even with those with whom we must deeply disagree, and this must someday be the basis of world peace and world law.

The fundamental task of our foreign-aid program is to help make an historical demonstration that economic growth and political democracy can develop hand in hand.

Partnership is not a posture but a process, a continuous process that grows stronger each year as we devote ourselves to common tasks.

We want a peace in which we can truly beat our swords into plowshares.

We seek not the worldwide victory of one nation or system, but a worldwide victory of men. The modern globe is too small, its weapons are too destructive, they multiply too fast, and its disorders are too contagious to permit any other kind of victory.

I run for the office of the Presidency not because I think it is an easy job in soft times. I think it is going to be the most difficult and hazardous year in our country's history. This is a time of danger.

Let every public servant know, whether his post is high or low, that a man's rank and reputation in this Administration will be determined by the size of the job he does, and not by the size of his staff, his office or his budget.

No government or social system is so evil that its people must be considered as lacking in virtue. As Americans, we find Communism profoundly repugnant as a negation of personal freedom and dignity. But we can still hail the Russian people for their many achievements — in science and space, in economic and industrial growth, in culture and in acts of courage.

What does truth require? It requires us to face the facts as they are, not to involve ourselves in self-destruction; to refuse to think merely in slogans.

The complacent, the self-indulgent, the soft societies are about to be swept away with the debris of history.

It is when the politician loves neither the public good nor himself, or when his love for himself is limited and is satisfied by the trappings of office, that the public interest is badly served. And it is when his regard for himself is so high that his own self-respect demands he follow the path of courage and conscience that all benefit.

Strong words alone, of course, do not make meaningful policy; they must, in foreign affairs in particular, be backed both by a will and by weapons that are equally strong. Thus a collection of Presidential statements cannot convey their true perspective unless it is realized or recalled precisely what they signified in committing the power and majesty of the American people and government.

In a democracy, every citizen, regardless of his interest in politics, "holds office"; every one of us is in a position of responsibility; and, in the final analysis, the kind of government we get depends upon how we fulfill those responsibilities. We, the people, are the boss, and we will get the kind of political leadership, be it good or bad, that we demand and deserve.

I sincerely believe that an American presidential

initiative for peace, honestly intended and reso-
lutely pursued, would not be lightly rejected by
either side. And I promise to waste no time in
taking this initiative.

Where else but in the political profession is the
individual expected to sacrifice all — including
his own career — for the national good?

The world was not meant to be a prison in which man awaits his execution. Nor has mankind survived the tests and trials of thousands of years to surrender everything, including its existence, now. This nation has the will and the faith to make a supreme effort to break the log jam on disarmament and nuclear tests; and we will persist until we prevail, until the rule of law has replaced the ever-dangerous use of force.

Until the world can develop a reliable system of international security, the free peoples have no choice but to keep their arms near.

We do not dismiss disarmament as an idle dream. For we believe in the end that it is the only way of insuring the security of all without impairing the interests of any. Nor do we mistake honorable negotiation for appeasement. While we shall never weary in the defense of freedom, neither shall we abandon the pursuit of peace.

First, let us examine our attitude toward peace itself. Too many of us think it is impossible. Too many think it unreal. But that is a dangerous, defeatist belief.

If we are to open new doorways to peace, if we

are to seize this rare opportunity for progress, if we are to be as bold and farsighted in our control of weapons as we have been in their invention, then let us now show all the world on this side of the wall and the other that a strong America also stands for peace.

We seek to strengthen the United Nations, to help solve its financial problems, to make it a more effective instrument of peace, to develop it into a genuine world security system capable of resolving disputes on the basis of law, of insuring the security of the large and small, and of creating conditions under which arms can finally be abolished.

Some say that it is useless to speak of world peace or world law or world disarmament, and that it will be useless until the leaders of the Soviet Union adopt a more enlightened attitude. I hope they do. I believe we can help them do it. But I also believe that we must reexamine our own attitude, as individuals and as a nation, for our attitude is as essential as theirs.

It is, I think a source of concern to us all that the first dogs carried around in outer space were not named Rover and Fido, but, instead, were named

Belka and Strelka. It was not named Checkers, either.

Together we shall save our planet or together we shall perish in its flames.

Disarmament without checks is but a shadow, and a community without law is but a shell.

Now it is time for a great new American enterprise, time for this nation to take a clearly leading role in space achievement, which in many ways may hold the key to our future on earth.

But why, some say, the moon? Why choose this as our goal? And they may well ask why climb the highest mountain? Why, 35 years ago, fly the Atlantic? Why does Rice play Texas?

Our arms will never be used to strike the first blow in any attack.

Remarks Prepared for Delivery at
The Trade Mart in Dallas, Texas,
November 22, 1963

We in this country, in this generation, are — by destiny rather than choice — the watchmen on the walls of world freedom. We ask, therefore, that we may be worthy of our strength with wisdom and restraint, and that we may achieve in our time and for all time the ancient vision of "peace on earth, good will toward men." That must always be our goal, and the righteousness of our cause must always underlie our strength. For as was written long ago: *except the Lord keep the city, the watchman waketh but in vain.*

ACKNOWLEDGMENTS

*Excerpts from the following are reprinted by permission
of Harper & Row, Publishers:*
PROFILES IN COURAGE *by John F. Kennedy
(Harper & Row, 1961).*

THE BURDEN AND THE GLORY, *edited by Allan Nevins
(Harper & Row, 1964).*
THE STRATEGY OF PEACE, *edited by Allan Nevins
(Harper & Row, 1960).*
TO TURN THE TIDE, *edited by John W. Gardner
(Harper & Row, 1962).*

Selections from AMERICA THE BEAUTIFUL IN THE WORDS OF
JOHN F. KENNEDY *by the Editors of Country Beautiful.
Copyright 1964 by Country Beautiful Foundation, Inc.,
Waukesha, Wisconsin.*

Selections from A THOUSAND DAYS, *by A. M. Schlesinger, Jr.,
Copyright 1965 by Houghton Mifflin Company.*

*In memory of John F. Kennedy
royalties from this book will be donated
to the Park Foundation.*

Designed by Harald Peter

Set in Linofilm Palatino, a 20th century typeface resembling a Venetian, designed by Hermann Zapf of Frankfurt. Printed on Hallmark Eggshell Book paper.